M000165109

FOR THE WORLD'S *Best* Dad

summersdale

FOR THE WORLD'S BEST DAD

This updated edition © Summersdale Publishers Ltd, 2021
First published in 2011 as *Bestest Dad Ever*
Published in 2016 as *Best Dad Ever*
Published in 2019 as *Dad in a Million*

An Hachette UK Company
www.hachette.co.uk

Summersdale Publishers Ltd
Part of Octopus Publishing Group Limited
Carmelite House
50 Victoria Embankment
LONDON
EC4Y 0DZ
UK

www.summersdale.com

Printed and bound in China

ISBN: 978-1-78783-656-3

Substantial discounts on bulk quantities of Summersdale books are available to corporations, professional associations and other organizations. For details contact general enquiries: telephone: +44 (0) 1243 771107 or email: enquiries@summersdale.com.

To......................................

From....................................

FAMILY IS NOT
AN IMPORTANT
THING. IT'S
EVERYTHING.

Michael J. Fox

MY FATHER GAVE ME THE
GREATEST GIFT ANYONE COULD
GIVE ANOTHER PERSON:
HE BELIEVED IN ME.

Jim Valvano

A FATHER
IS A GIANT
FROM WHOSE
SHOULDERS YOU
CAN SEE FOREVER.

Perry Garfinkel

DAD TAUGHT ME
EVERYTHING I KNOW.
UNFORTUNATELY,
HE DIDN'T TEACH
ME EVERYTHING
HE KNOWS.

Al Unser Jr

A truly rich man is
one whose children run
into his arms when his
hands are empty.

NOBLE FATHERS HAVE
NOBLE CHILDREN.

Euripides

My dad is my hero... I'm never free of a problem, nor do I truly experience a joy until we share it.

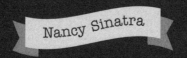

Nancy Sinatra

My father didn't tell me
how to live; he lived, and
let me watch him do it.

CLARENCE BUDINGTON KELLAND

What do I owe my father? Everything.

HENRY van DYKE

I LOVE MY FATHER AS
THE STARS — HE'S A BRIGHT
SHINING EXAMPLE AND
A HAPPY TWINKLING
IN MY HEART.

Terri Guillemets

Things dads can do with one hand behind their back

CARRY THE FAMILY'S LUGGAGE (INCLUDING THREE POOL FLOATS AND A DECKCHAIR)

RESCUE A FAVOURITE BALL FROM
THE NEIGHBOUR'S GUTTERING

FIND A PARKING SPOT IN THE
BUSIEST OF CAR PARKS

CARRY SLEEPING CHILDREN UP TO
BED WITHOUT WAKING THEM

FIX A BROKEN TOY (ESPECIALLY
REATTACHING BODY PARTS TO
ACTION FIGURES AND DOLLS)

MAKE A DEN IN THE GARDEN WITH
OLD JUNK FROM THE SHED

SMUGGLE CHOCOLATE
BARS OUT OF THE KITCHEN
WITHOUT ANYONE SEEING

SIMULTANEOUSLY DRINK
BEER, EAT SNACKS AND KEEP
OTHER PEOPLE'S HANDS AWAY
FROM THE TV REMOTE

WHEN I WAS A KID,
I USED TO IMAGINE
ANIMALS RUNNING
UNDER MY BED. I TOLD
MY DAD... HE CUT THE
LEGS OFF THE BED.

Lou Brock

Dads are stone skimmers, mud wallowers, water wallopers, ceiling swoopers, shoulder gallopers, upsy-downsy, over-and-through, round-and-about whooshers.

HELEN THOMSON

My dad is truly the best.
He is everything a father
should be and the greatest
man I will ever know.

Dakota Fanning

HAVING ONE
CHILD MAKES
YOU A PARENT;
HAVING TWO,
YOU ARE A
REFEREE.

David Frost

ASK YOUR MOTHER.

Frank Lancaster's advice
to his children

MY DADDY,
HE WAS SOMEWHERE
BETWEEN GOD AND
JOHN WAYNE.

Hank Williams Jr

"

The raising
of a child is
the building of
a cathedral.
You can't cut
corners.

DAVE EGGERS

"

A FATHER'S
SMILE HAS
BEEN KNOWN
TO LIGHT UP
A CHILD'S
ENTIRE DAY.

Susan Gale

**FATHERING IS
NOT SOMETHING
PERFECT MEN DO,
BUT SOMETHING THAT
PERFECTS THE MAN.**

Frank Pittman

ONE FATHER
IS MORE THAN
A HUNDRED
SCHOOLMASTERS.

George Herbert

SOMETIMES THE POOREST MAN
LEAVES HIS CHILDREN THE
RICHEST INHERITANCE.

Ruth E. Renkel

You know you're a dad when...

... YOU CAN FINISH YOUR OWN MEAL, PLUS LEFTOVERS, AND STILL MAKE ROOM FOR ONE OR TWO OF YOUR CHILDREN'S DESSERTS

... YOU REMAIN CONFIDENT IN YOUR NAVIGATION SKILLS, EVEN WHEN IT'S OBVIOUS YOU'RE COMPLETELY LOST

... YOU COME BACK WITH A 12-PACK OF BEER AND A FAMILY-SIZE BAR OF CHOCOLATE WHEN ASKED TO DO THE WEEKLY SHOP

... YOUR CHILD COMING THIRD
IN THE WHEELBARROW RACE IS
AS IMPORTANT AS YOUR TEAM
WINNING THE WORLD CUP

~

... YOU'RE NOT EMBARRASSED TO
SING (THE WRONG WORDS) TO A
HIP NEW SONG ON THE RADIO

... YOU CAN'T RESIST THE URGE TO PROVE THAT YOU'VE "STILL GOT IT" AT ANY FAMILY EVENT INVOLVING A DANCEFLOOR

... YOU ALWAYS VOLUNTEER TO HELP WITH HOMEWORK — EVEN THOUGH YOU HAVE NO IDEA WHAT A FRONTAL ADVERBIAL IS

It's the most profound
gift and the most
daunting challenge.

Matt Bomer on fatherhood

A HAPPY FAMILY IS
BUT AN EARLIER HEAVEN.

George Bernard Shaw

You don't raise heroes,
you raise sons. And if you
treat them like sons, they'll
turn out to be heroes.

WALTER M. SCHIRRA SR

ANYONE WHO TELLS
YOU FATHERHOOD IS
THE GREATEST THING
THAT CAN HAPPEN
TO YOU, THEY ARE
UNDERSTATING IT.

Mike Myers

I HAVE FOUND THE BEST WAY
TO GIVE ADVICE TO YOUR
CHILDREN IS TO FIND OUT
WHAT THEY WANT AND THEN
ADVISE THEM TO DO IT.

Harry S. Truman

"

My mother gave me my drive, but my father gave me my dreams.

LIZA MINNELLI

THERE'S NOTHING
THAT MAKES YOU
MORE INSANE
THAN FAMILY.
OR MORE HAPPY.

Jim Butcher

Your dad is the man
who does all the heavy
shovelling for your
sandcastle and then
tells you you've done
a wonderful job.

Rose O'Kelly

Whoever does not talk to
his father never knows
what his grandfather said.

PAUL RUSESABAGINA

MY DAD: ONE OF THE WISEST,
MOST AUTHENTIC, INTEGRITY-
FILLED, HEARTFUL PEOPLE
I'VE EVER KNOWN. HE SHAPED
ME INTO WHO I AM.

Connie Britton

What we become depends
on what our fathers
teach us at odd moments,
when they aren't
trying to teach us.

Umberto Eco

OTHER THINGS MAY CHANGE US, BUT WE START AND END WITH THE FAMILY.

Anthony Brandt

Things that always make a dad proud

TAKING THE TRAINING WHEELS OFF THE BIKE (EVEN IF HE HAS TO PUT THEM STRAIGHT BACK ON AGAIN)

WATCHING THEM TIE THEIR OWN
SHOELACES (EVEN IF SOME
FINGERS GET TIED IN THEM TOO)

SEEING THEM IN THE SCHOOL
NATIVITY PLAY (EVEN IF THEY
DID ONLY PLAY SHEEP #6)

CONGRATULATING THEM ON A GOOD GRADE FOR THEIR HOMEWORK ASSIGNMENT (EVEN IF HE DID MOST OF THE WORK)

SEEING THEM MENTIONED IN THE LOCAL PAPER (EVEN IF IT WAS FOR COMING NEXT TO LAST IN THE CHURCH TALENT SHOW)

ATTENDING THEIR GRADUATION
(EVEN IF HE STILL HAS NO CLUE
WHAT THEY WERE STUDYING)

SEEING THEM PASS THEIR
DRIVING TEST (EVEN IF IT DID
DRAIN HIS BANK ACCOUNT)

WATCHING THEM MOVE INTO THEIR OWN PLACE (EVEN IF THEY DO TAKE HALF OF THE HOUSEHOLD APPLIANCES WITH THEM)

DAD ALWAYS CALLED ME HIS "FAVOURITE SON".

Cameron Diaz on being a tomboy

BY THE TIME A MAN REALIZES
THAT MAYBE HIS FATHER WAS
RIGHT, HE USUALLY HAS A SON
WHO THINKS HE'S WRONG.

Charles Wadsworth

"

A father is a banker provided by nature.

FRENCH PROVERB

"

Lately, all my friends
are worried that they're
turning into their fathers.
I'm worried that I'm not.

DAN ZEVIN

MY DAD'S PANTS
KEPT CREEPING UP
ON HIM. BY 65 HE
WAS JUST A PAIR OF
PANTS AND A HEAD.

Jeff Altman

IT IS A WISE
FATHER THAT
KNOWS HIS
OWN CHILD.

William Shakespeare

IT IS
MUCH EASIER
TO BECOME A
FATHER THAN
TO BE ONE.

Kent Nerburn

NO MAN I EVER MET
WAS MY FATHER'S
EQUAL, AND I NEVER
LOVED ANY OTHER
MAN AS MUCH.

Hedy Lamarr

THE HEART OF A
FATHER IS THE
MASTERPIECE
OF NATURE.

Antoine François
Prévost d'Exiles

It's the courage to raise a child that makes you a father.

BARACK OBAMA

I cannot think of any
need in childhood as
strong as the need for
a father's protection.

SIGMUND FREUD

Ways dad will always embarrass his children

HE'LL GIVE THEM A KISS
ON THE CHEEK IN FRONT OF
THEIR FRIENDS WHEN HE
DROPS THEM OFF AT SCHOOL

HE'LL TRY TO SOUND COOL WITH
DODGY REFERENCES TO POPULAR
CULTURE... "ANYONE HEARD THE
NEW BARRY STYLES ALBUM?"

HE'LL TELL JOKES THAT
ONLY HE FINDS FUNNY

HE'LL TELL THEM "CRAZY" STORIES FROM HIS YOUTH, WAITING FOR THEM TO TELL HIM HE'S COOL

... OR HE'LL TELL THEM ALL ABOUT THE TIME YOU HAD TO SLEEP WITH THE LIGHT ON AFTER WATCHING *JURASSIC PARK*

HE'LL WEAR SOMETHING THAT
STOPPED FITTING HIM 20 YEARS
AGO — IN PUBLIC, OF COURSE

HE'LL PHOTOBOMB EVERY
PICTURE THEY TAKE

HE'LL CONTINUE TO REFER
TO THEM AS "PUMPKIN",
"SUNSHINE" OR ANY OTHER
SUCH CHILDHOOD NICKNAME
UNTIL THEY'RE AT LEAST 40

A FATHER IS THE ONE FRIEND UPON WHOM WE CAN ALWAYS RELY.

Émile Gaboriau

My father is my rock.
It's where I learned
everything about loyalty,
dependability, being
there day in, day out,
no matter what.

HUGH JACKMAN

I THINK MY DAD IS
A LOT COOLER THAN
OTHER DADS. HE STILL
ACTS LIKE HE'S 17.

Miley Cyrus

66

The sooner you treat your son as a man, the sooner he will be one.

JOHN DRYDEN

99

THERE IS MORE
TO FATHERS THAN
MEETS THE EYE.

Margaret Atwood

ONLY A
FATHER DOESN'T
BEGRUDGE HIS
SON'S TALENT.

Johann Wolfgang von Goethe

TO HER, THE
NAME OF FATHER
WAS ANOTHER
NAME FOR LOVE.

Fanny Fern

YOU CAN'T UNDERSTAND IT
UNTIL YOU EXPERIENCE THE
SIMPLE JOY OF THE FIRST
TIME YOUR SON POINTS AT A
SEAGULL AND SAYS "DUCK".

Russell Crowe on fatherhood

"

The secret of fatherhood is to know when to stop tickling.

ANONYMOUS

**BLESSED INDEED IS
THE MAN WHO HEARS
MANY GENTLE VOICES
CALL HIM FATHER.**

Lydia Maria Child

THERE'S NO PILLOW
QUITE SO SOFT AS A
FATHER'S STRONG
SHOULDER.

Richard L. Evans

Secret skills that only dads know

HOW TO ASSEMBLE ANYTHING, EVEN WITH JAPANESE INSTRUCTIONS (WHO READS INSTRUCTIONS ANYWAY?!)

HOW TO LOSE CONVINCINGLY
AT EVERY SINGLE GAME HE
PLAYS WITH HIS CHILDREN

———

HOW TO FIX STROLLERS...
AND BIKES... AND CARS

HOW TO FOLLOW A FILM'S PLOT
LINE, DESPITE HAVING SLEPT
THROUGH THE WHOLE THING

HOW TO PULL OFF THE
"SOCKS, SANDALS AND SUNBURN"
LOOK (WELL, SORT OF)

HOW TO CALL EVERYONE
TO THE DINNER TABLE,
EVEN IF THEY'RE PLAYING
AT THE END OF THE STREET

HOW TO BREAK WIND AND BLAME
IT ON THE DOG/CAT/HAMSTER

I realized being a father
is the greatest job I have
ever had and the greatest
job I will ever have.

Dwayne Johnson

THE HARDEST PART OF MY NEW
LIFE AS A DAD IS LEAVING
FOR WORK IN THE MORNING.

Mario Lopez

"Father" is the noblest
title a man can be given...
It signifies a patriarch,
a leader, an exemplar,
a confidant, a teacher,
a hero, a friend.

Robert L. Backman

It's only when you grow up and step back from him – or leave him for your own home – it's only then that you can measure his greatness and fully appreciate it.

MARGARET TRUMAN

TELLING A TEENAGER THE FACTS OF LIFE IS LIKE GIVING A FISH A BATH.

Arnold H. Glasow

BEING A GREAT FATHER IS
LIKE SHAVING. NO MATTER
HOW GOOD YOU SHAVED
TODAY, YOU HAVE TO DO
IT AGAIN TOMORROW.

Reed Markham

When I was a kid, I said to my father one afternoon, "Daddy, will you take me to the zoo?" He answered, "If the zoo wants you, let them come and get you."

JERRY LEWIS

A father is a man who expects his son to be as good as he meant to be.

FRANK A. CLARK

THE FAMILY IS ONE OF
NATURE'S MASTERPIECES.

George Santayana

I HAVEN'T TAUGHT
PEOPLE IN 50 YEARS
WHAT MY FATHER
TAUGHT BY EXAMPLE
IN ONE WEEK.

Mario Cuomo

Awards for "the world's best dad"

BRAVERY IN THE FACE
OF SPIDERS AND OTHER
INTIMIDATING CREATURES

FRIENDLIEST 24-HOUR
TAXI DRIVER

BEST SEAN CONNERY
IMPRESSION

CHAMPION PANCAKE FLIPPER

BIGGEST BEAR HUGS

LOUDEST FOOTBALL SUPPORTER

MAKER OF THE TASTIEST
BACON SANDWICH

LORD OF THE (DAD) DANCE

~

PREMIER PRANKSTER

BEST CORNY JOKE TELLER

BEST ADVICE GIVER

BEING A DAD IS
MORE IMPORTANT
THAN FOOTBALL,
MORE IMPORTANT
THAN ANYTHING.

David Beckham

FATHER, DAD, PAPA — NO MATTER WHAT YOU CALL THEM, THEY INFLUENCE OUR LIVES AND THEY ARE THE PERSON WE LOOK UP TO.

Catherine Pulsifer

MY FATHER USED
TO SAY THAT
IT'S NEVER TOO
LATE TO DO
ANYTHING YOU
WANTED TO DO.

Michael Jordan

LIFE DOESN'T
COME WITH AN
INSTRUCTION
BOOK. THAT'S
WHY WE HAVE
FATHERS.

H. Jackson Brown Jr

HE OPENED THE JAR
OF PICKLES WHEN NO
ONE ELSE COULD.

Erma Bombeck
on her dad

THERE IS A
SPECIAL PLACE
IN HEAVEN FOR THE
FATHER WHO TAKES
HIS DAUGHTER
SHOPPING.

John Sinor

Character is largely caught, and the father and the home should be the great sources of character infection.

FRANK H. CHELEY

GETTING A BURP
OUT OF YOUR
LITTLE THING
IS PROBABLY
THE GREATEST
SATISFACTION I'VE
COME ACROSS.

Brad Pitt on his first child

"

My father, he was like the rock, the guy you went to with every problem.

GWYNETH PALTROW

Dads regard themselves
as giant shock absorbers,
there to protect the family
from the ruts and bumps
on the road of life.

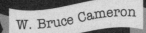

W. Bruce Cameron

Dads are most ordinary
men turned by love into
heroes, adventurers, story-
tellers, and singers of song.

PAM BROWN

IT HAS GIVEN
ME PURPOSE,
TAUGHT ME
PATIENCE AND
EXPANDED
MY HEART.

Neil Patrick Harris
on fatherhood

You never get really cross, even when...

... I LEAVE JUNK ALL
OVER THE CAR SEATS

... I FLOOD THE BATHROOM
AFTER LEAVING THE TAP
RUNNING (AGAIN)

... I CHANGE THE TEMPERATURE
ON THE THERMOSTAT WITHOUT
ASKING YOU FIRST

... I USE YOUR FAVOURITE
FOOTBALL SHIRT TO WIPE
THE DOG DOWN AFTER A
PARTICULARLY MUDDY WALK

... MY STRAIGHTENERS BURN A
HOLE IN THE CARPET

... I SEEM INCAPABLE OF
ADJUSTING THE VOLUME
OF MY SPEAKERS

... I CALL YOU AT 3 A.M. TO COME
AND PICK ME UP FROM A PARTY

... I COME HOME WITH A NOSE
RING AND THE CAST OF *STRANGER
THINGS* TATTOOED ON MY BACK

I ENCOURAGE ALL
FATHERS TO FOCUS
ON THE INTANGIBLES,
BECAUSE THOSE ARE
THE GIFTS THAT MAKE
THE DIFFERENCE.

Asha Patrick

A DAD IS SOMEONE WHO
WANTS TO CATCH YOU BEFORE
YOU FALL, BUT INSTEAD PICKS
YOU UP, BRUSHES YOU OFF
AND LETS YOU TRY AGAIN.

Anonymous

While we try to teach our children all about life, our children teach us what life is all about.

ANGELA SCHWINDT

**THEIR ABSOLUTE LOVE
OF THEIR CHILDREN
PLACES THEM ABOVE
THE HIGHEST PRAISE.**

Anton Chekhov talking
about his parents

THERE'S NOTHING MORE
CONTAGIOUS THAN THE
DIGNITY OF A FATHER.

Amit Ray

MY FATHER HAD
A PROFOUND
INFLUENCE ON
ME – HE WAS
A LUNATIC.

Spike Milligan

IT WAS MY FATHER
WHO TAUGHT ME TO
VALUE MYSELF.

Dawn French

No man can possibly
know what life means,
what the world means,
until he has a child
and loves it.

LAFCADIO HEARN

WHEN MY FATHER
DIDN'T HAVE MY
HAND, HE HAD
MY BACK.

Linda Poindexter

66

My father was my teacher. But most importantly he was a great dad.

BEAU BRIDGES

99

FAMILY IS THE MOST IMPORTANT THING IN THE WORLD.

Diana, Princess of Wales

Things found in dad's shed

AN OBSOLETE GAMING
CONSOLE (OR THREE)

TWELVE GALLONS OF
UNTOUCHED HOME BREW FROM
A COUPLE OF YEARS BACK

A MANUAL FOR A CAR
HE SOLD 15 YEARS AGO

THE FIRST CHAPTER OF A
BOOK-IN-PROGRESS ENTITLED
101 USES FOR DEAD BATTERIES

———

THE NOVELTY TIE HE
GOT FROM GRANDMA AT
CHRISTMAS LAST YEAR

HIS PRIZED
BEER-BOTTLE-TOP
COLLECTION

A FAILED ATTEMPT AT A "BUILD
YOUR OWN" CRYSTAL RADIO

THE SPORTS KIT HE WORE
WHEN HE WAS AT SCHOOL

I take pride in knowing
that of all the things I have
accomplished, no success
or honour is greater than
that of being a father.

Les Brown

[MY FATHER] WAS VERY IMPORTANT TO ME, BECAUSE HE MADE ME THINK.

Janis Joplin

You have your time set aside for being a rock 'n' roll star... Then there's going to have to be times set aside for being daddy and having chocolate rubbed in my face.

NOEL GALLAGHER

MY DAD ALWAYS HAD THIS
LITTLE SIGN ON HIS DESK:
"THE BIGGER YOUR HEAD
IS, THE EASIER YOUR
SHOES ARE TO FILL."

Phil Jackson

NO LOVE IS
GREATER THAN
THAT OF A
FATHER FOR
HIS SON.

Dan Brown

YOU WILL ALWAYS
BE YOUR CHILD'S
FAVOURITE TOY.

Vicki Lansky

"

*My father's busy
but he always has
time for me.*

JUDY BLUME

"

RAISING KIDS IS
PART JOY AND PART
GUERRILLA WARFARE.

Ed Asner

It is amazing how
quickly the kids learn
to drive a car, yet are
unable to understand
the lawnmower...
or vacuum cleaner.

BEN BERGOR

I LOVE MY DAD, ALTHOUGH I'M
DEFINITELY CRITICAL OF HIM
SOMETIMES, LIKE WHEN HIS
PANTS ARE TOO TIGHT.

Liv Tyler

HOW SWEET 'TIS TO SIT 'NEATH A FOND FATHER'S SMILE.

John Howard Payne

You're the best dad because...

—

... YOU GO ON ALL THE RIDES AT
THE FAIR AND DON'T COMPLAIN
WHEN YOU FEEL SICK

... YOU NEVER ASK FOR THAT
MONEY I "BORROWED"

... YOU'RE ALWAYS PROUD
OF MY ACHIEVEMENTS

... YOU GIVE THE WARMEST HUGS

... YOU ALWAYS BARBECUE MY
BURGER TO PERFECTION

... YOU'RE ALWAYS THERE FOR ME

... YOU LET ME MAKE
MY OWN MISTAKES

... YOU ALWAYS MAKE ME LAUGH
(EVEN WHEN YOUR JOKES
ARE TERRIBLE)

My father once said,
"If the whole world wants
to go left and you feel like
going right, go right. You
don't have to follow."

Yanni

FATHER! – TO GOD
HIMSELF WE CANNOT
GIVE A HOLIER NAME.

William Wordsworth

"

Children learn to smile from their parents.

SHINICHI SUZUKI

"

NOTHING COULD
GET AT ME IF I
CURLED UP ON MY
FATHER'S LAP...
ALL ABOUT HIM
WAS SAFE.

Naomi Mitchison

IT WAS INTO MY
FATHER'S IMAGE...
THAT I'D PACKED ALL
THE ATTRIBUTES I
SOUGHT IN MYSELF.

Barack Obama

You don't choose
your family. They are
God's gift to you, as
you are to them.

DESMOND TUTU

THE BEST WAY TO MAKE
CHILDREN GOOD IS TO
MAKE THEM HAPPY.

Oscar Wilde

YOUR CHILDREN
NEED YOUR PRESENCE
MORE THAN YOUR
PRESENTS.

Jesse Jackson

I have always had the
feeling I could do anything
and my dad told me I could.

Ann Richards

THERE'S NO SUBSTITUTE FOR A FULL-TIME DAD.

Tony Dungy

"

The mark of
a good parent
is that he can
have fun while
being one.

MARCELENE COX

"

Thank you
for being...

... the world's
best dad!

If you're interested in finding out
more about our books, find us on Facebook
at **Summersdale Publishers** and follow us
on Twitter at **@Summersdale**.

www.summersdale.com

Image credits

pp.9, 19, 27, 37, 55, 67, 76, 98, 115, 121, 136, 141, 151,
156, 160 © Ps_Ai/Shutterstock.com; pp.10, 21, 34,
41, 44, 82, 84, 107, 131, 147, 155 © mStudioVector/
Shutterstock.com; pp.14, 30, 46, 62, 78, 92, 126,
142, 159 © Mischoko/Shutterstock.com